Textures

Written by Paul Bennett

Wayland

CRISS✗CROSS

Bodies	Fairgrounds	Light	Special Days
Boxes	Growth	Patterns	Textures
Changes	Holes	Rubbish	Weather
Colours	Journeys	Senses	Wheels

Picture acknowledgements

The publishers would like to thank the following for allowing their photographs to be reproduced in this book: Bruce Coleman Ltd 7 (Jane Burton), 11 (above/Hans Reinhard), 21 (above/Kim Taylor), 23 (above/George McCarthy); Chris Fairclough Colour Library 14, 20, 23 (below), 27 (both); Tizzie Knowles *title page*, 15 (below), 17 (above), 25; Reflections 5 (below/Jennie Woodcock), 13 (Jennie Woodcock); Skjold 6 (above); Topham 28, 29 (above); Eye Ubiquitous 8 (below/Paul Thompson), 15 (above/Mostyn), 16 (Roger Chester); Wayland Picture Library 4, 5 (above), 6 (below), 9 (bottom/left), 12 (below), 26 (both); Tim Woodcock 9 (main picture), 10 (both), 17 (below), 21 (below), 24 (above); ZEFA 8 (above), 11 (below), 18, 19 (below), 22, 24 (below).

Cover photography by Daniel Pangbourne, organized by Zoë Hargreaves. With thanks to the Fox Primary School. A special thank you to Hebe and Charlie.

First published in 1993 by
Wayland (Publishers) Ltd
61 Western Road, Hove
East Sussex BN3 1JD, England

© Copyright 1993 Wayland (Publishers) Ltd

Editor: Francesca Motisi
Designer: Jean Wheeler

Consultant: Alison Watkins is an experienced teacher with a special interest in language and reading. She has been a class teacher and the special needs coordinator for a school in Hackney. Alison wrote the notes for parents and teachers and provided the topic web.

British Library Cataloguing in Publication Data
Bennett, Paul.
Textures. – (Criss Cross)
I. Title II. Series
620.1

ISBN 0-7502-0512-1

Typeset by DJS Fotoset Ltd, Brighton, Sussex
Printed and bound in Italy by L.E.G.O. S.p.A., Vicenza

Contents

Words printed in **bold** in the text are explained in the glossary on page 32.

What things feel like

Texture is what something feels like when you touch it. Rabbits feel soft, which makes them nice to stroke. Do you have a pet with soft fur?

4

Feel many different things. A piece of wood and a metal spoon are smooth and hard, while sandpaper is rough. What do you think the white block of **polystyrene** feels like?

Ice-cream is cold and soft. It can be sticky too!

5

Rough

Tree trunks feel very rough. They are covered with bumpy bark. Do you have a favourite tree that you can climb?

Bricks are rough. If you slipped climbing up a wall, you might graze your knees.

The skin of this African elephant has many
wrinkles and folds. What do you think its skin
would feel like if you could touch it?

Smooth

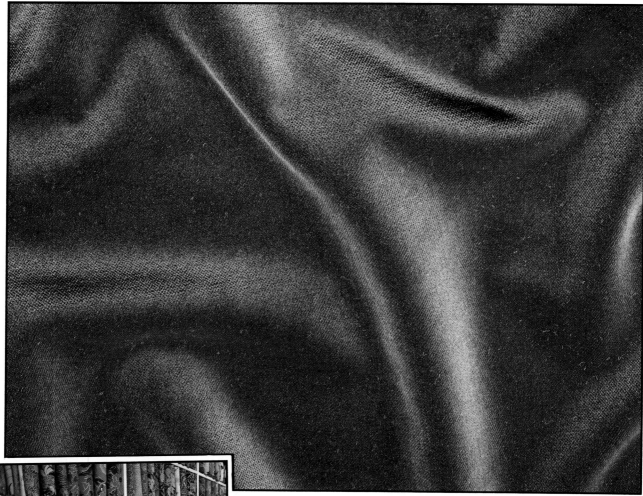

8

Have you heard the saying, *as smooth as silk*? Silk cloth is made from the very fine **threads** spun by **silkworms**. What else can you find at home that is as smooth as silk?

There are no wrinkles or bumps
on a slide. The smooth surface
helps you to go faster.
Can you think why?

These children
are stroking a horse.
Its coat is very smooth.

Soft

Many toys are soft and fluffy. What does your favourite cuddly toy feel like?

Clay is a soft earth that is used to make **pottery**.

10

The feathers of baby birds are called down. These ducklings are very soft to touch. Have you ever held a real duckling, or a fluffy toy duckling?

Hard

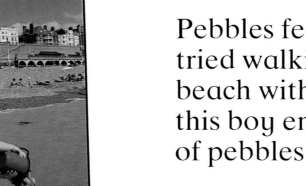

Pebbles feel hard. Have you tried walking on a pebbly beach with bare feet? When this boy empties his bucket of pebbles, they bounce!

Pots and pans feel hard. These are made from a kind of metal called aluminium.

Crash helmets are hard on the outside. People wear them to **protect** their heads, in case they fall off a pony, bicycle or motorbike. Can you think of any other people who need to wear crash helmets?

13

Sharp

Many plants have
spikes on them.
◀ Rose thorns
have sharp points
that can prick you
like a needle if
you touch them.

Teasels have prickly
leaves, stems and
heads. ▶

Knives are sharp. They
are dangerous because
they can cut you. Never
touch or play with sharp
things. Let a grown-up
help you when you want
to do some cooking.

15

Do you have a baby brother or sister?
Toys for the very young have blunt edges.
Can you guess why?

16

This boy is holding a blunt pencil. What makes your pencils blunt?

This girl is using a pair of round-nosed scissors. They are safe to use because they are not pointed at the ends.

Rubbery

Rubbery things can stretch or bend.
Wellington boots feel rubbery.

Many balls are made from rubber. If you drop a rubber ball, it will bounce.

Bouncy castles feel rubbery. You can have fun jumping on them.

19

Sticky

Plasters and Sellotape are sticky.
What else do you have at home that is sticky?

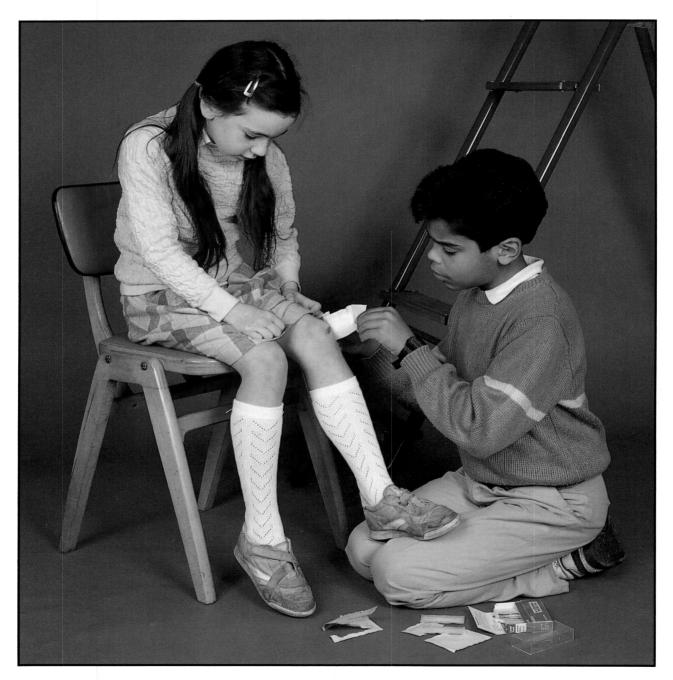

This sundew plant
has leaves covered
with sticky hairs.
When an insect
lands on the plant, it
becomes stuck and
cannot fly away.

Glue is sticky.
You can use it to
stick things together.

Slimy

Things that are slimy feel soft and are a bit runny. The white of this egg is slimy.

Slugs are slimy. You can tell where a slug has been from its slime trail.

Frogs lay eggs called spawn. It looks like jelly but is very slimy. The black dots will grow into tadpoles and then frogs.

Itchy and tickly

Long grass can tickle your skin.

A feather is soft
and smooth.
It is tickly too.

24

Some people do not like to wear wool next to their skin because it makes them itch. Do you have some clothes that make you itch when you wear them?

Changing texture

This girl is having a **cast** made from **plaster of Paris** to support her broken arm. The cast is soft while it is wet, but it soon becomes hard when it dries.

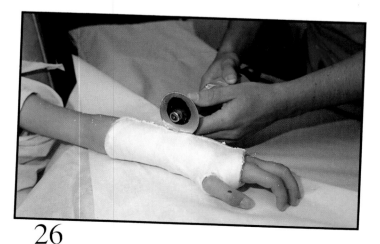

When the broken arm has mended, the cast is removed with a special tool.

The texture of food changes when it is cooked. Cakes are very different before and after they are cooked.

Dripping water freezes when it is very cold.
It turns into hard icicles like these.

In cold, frosty weather, the ground is hard. But when the weather gets warmer, the ground becomes soft again. Do you know why?

Notes for parents and teachers

Science
- Children should collect and find similarities and differences in a variety of everyday materials, natural and manufactured.
- Ask children to set up a fair test to find out which material is best at not wearing out when rubbed against a rough surface. Try a variety of materials and surfaces.
- What happens when foods such as ice-cubes and chocolate are left at room temperature? Leave in different places and record changes. Also discuss with the children hygiene implications here.
- Set up a special table or board where children can bring in things with interesting textures.
- Children should have lots of tactile play and experiences with things that run through their fingers. Try dry lentils, peas, rice, pasta, shaving foam, hair gel. Also try cotton wool, sandpaper, velvet, feathers, bubble wrap, different brushes and textured wallpaper. This will also help to develop children's fine motor skills and coordination.

Mathematics
- Make 'feely' numbers out of sandpaper etc. This helps children to grasp the shape and directionality of numbers. Make it into a guessing game.
- Use tactile materials to teach shapes.

Language
- At this level the relationship between language and other curriculum areas is crucial and we rely heavily upon spoken language. Children need to be encouraged to talk about what they are doing and observing. Every opportunity for the children to express their thinking and interact orally with each other should be seized upon.
- Make a 'feely' alphabet. Play lotto, bingo or pairs using the letters.

Art
- Children can experiment with a wide range of media to produce various effects. Charcoal, paints, oil pastels, chalks, wax crayons etc.
- They can also experiment and work with various types of paper or card. Try bubbled textured paper, frosted, glossy, shiny and mat-surfaced paper. Embossed paper is easy to cut and provides an interesting surface for printing and spraying with metallic paint, and corrugated paper can be rolled to make free-standing models.
- Use a camera to record interesting and various textures.
- Add p.v.a. glue to paint to create a thick paste suitable for a more textured effect.

History/Geography
- Go on a walkabout in your local environment. Look for clues about its history by taking rubbings and using evidence.

*The theme textures can stand on its own but could also be a part of other topics such as materials, clothes, food, pattern, minibeasts, plants, animals or buildings.

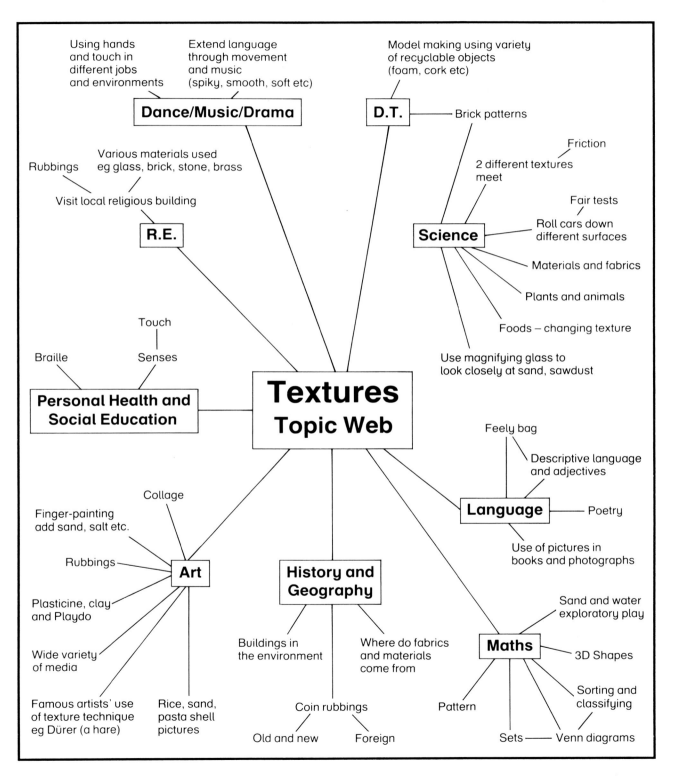

Using hands
and touch in
different jobs
and environments

Extend language
through movement
and music
(spiky, smooth, soft etc)

Model making using variety
of recyclable objects
(foam, cork etc)

Dance/Music/Drama

D.T. —— Brick patterns

Friction

2 different textures
meet

Rubbings

Various materials used
eg glass, brick, stone, brass

Visit local religious building

Fair tests

Roll cars down
different surfaces

R.E.

Science

Materials and fabrics

Plants and animals

Foods – changing texture

Touch

Use magnifying glass to
look closely at sand, sawdust

Braille

Senses

**Personal Health and
Social Education**

Textures
Topic Web

Feely bag

Descriptive language
and adjectives

Language —— Poetry

Use of pictures in
books and photographs

Collage

Finger-painting
add sand, salt etc.

Rubbings ——

Art

Plasticine, clay
and Playdo

Wide variety
of media

Famous artists' use
of texture technique
eg Dürer (a hare)

Rice, sand,
pasta shell
pictures

**History and
Geography**

Buildings in
the environment

Where do fabrics
and materials
come from

Sand and water
exploratory play

Maths

3D Shapes

Sorting and
classifying

Pattern

Coin rubbings

Old and new   Foreign

Sets —— Venn diagrams

31

Glossary

Cast   The plaster support for a broken arm or leg.

Plaster of Paris   A white powder that is used for making casts for setting broken arms and legs.

Polystyrene   A white, hard foam used for packing.

Pottery   Objects made from baked clay.

Protect   To stop something from being hurt.

Silkworms   Caterpillars that spin silk cocoons.

Teasels   Types of prickly plants.

Threads   Fine strands or fibres of material.

Wrinkles   Creases or folds.

Index